LAYERS OF LEARNING
YEAR TWO • UNIT FIVE

ANGLO-SAXONS
BRITAIN
WILD WEATHER
KING ARTHUR TALES

Published by HooDoo Publishing
United States of America
© 2014 Layers of Learning
Copies of maps or activities may be made for a particular family or classroom.
ISBN 978-1495296031

Units At A Glance: Topics For All Four Years of the Layers of Learning Program

1	History	Geography	Science	The Arts
1	Mesopotamia	Maps & Globes	Planets	Cave Paintings
2	Egypt	Map Keys	Stars	Egyptian Art
3	Europe	Global Grids	Earth & Moon	Crafts
4	Ancient Greece	Wonders	Satellites	Greek Art
5	Babylon	Mapping People	Humans in Space	Poetry
6	The Levant	Physical Earth	Laws of Motion	List Poems
7	Phoenicians	Oceans	Motion	Moral Stories
8	Assyrians	Deserts	Fluids	Rhythm
9	Persians	Arctic	Waves	Melody
10	Ancient China	Forests	Machines	Chinese Art
11	Early Japan	Mountains	States of Matter	Line & Shape
12	Arabia	Rivers & Lakes	Atoms	Color & Value
13	Ancient India	Grasslands	Elements	Texture & Form
14	Ancient Africa	Africa	Bonding	African Tales
15	First North Americans	North America	Salts	Creative Kids
16	Ancient South America	South America	Plants	South American Art
17	Celts	Europe	Flowering Plants	Jewelry
18	Roman Republic	Asia	Trees	Roman Art
19	Christianity	Australia & Oceania	Simple Plants	Instruments
20	Roman Empire	You Explore	Fungi	Composing Music

2	History	Geography	Science	The Arts
1	Byzantines	Turkey	Climate & Seasons	Byzantine Art
2	Barbarians	Ireland	Forecasting	Illumination
3	Islam	Arabian Peninsula	Clouds & Precipitation	Creative Kids
4	Vikings	Norway	Special Effects	Viking Art
5	Anglo Saxons	Britain	Wild Weather	King Arthur Tales
6	Charlemagne	France	Cells and DNA	Carolingian Art
7	Normans	Nigeria	Skeletons	Canterbury Tales
8	Feudal System	Germany	Muscles, Skin, & Cardiopulmonary	Gothic Art
9	Crusades	Balkans	Digestive & Senses	Religious Art
10	Burgundy, Venice, Spain	Switzerland	Nerves	Oil Paints
11	Wars of the Roses	Russia	Health	Minstrels & Plays
12	Eastern Europe	Hungary	Metals	Printmaking
13	African Kingdoms	Mali	Carbon Chem	Textiles
14	Asian Kingdoms	Southeast Asia	Non-metals	Vivid Language
15	Mongols	Caucasus	Gases	Fun With Poetry
16	Medieval China & Japan	China	Electricity	Asian Arts
17	Pacific Peoples	Micronesia	Circuits	Arts of the Islands
18	American Peoples	Canada	Technology	Indian Legends
19	The Renaissance	Italy	Magnetism	Renaissance Art I
20	Explorers	Caribbean Sea	Motors	Renaissance Art II

3	History	Geography	Science	The Arts
1	Age of Exploration	Argentina and Chile	Classification & Insects	Fairy Tales
2	The Ottoman Empire	Egypt and Libya	Reptiles & Amphibians	Poetry
3	Mogul Empire	Pakistan & Afghanistan	Fish	Mogul Arts
4	Reformation	Angola & Zambia	Birds	Reformation Art
5	Renaissance England	Tanzania & Kenya	Mammals & Primates	Shakespeare
6	Thirty Years' War	Spain	Sound	Baroque Music
7	The Dutch	Netherlands	Light & Optics	Baroque Art I
8	France	Indonesia	Bending Light	Baroque Art II
9	The Enlightenment	Korean Pen.	Color	Art Journaling
10	Russia & Prussia	Central Asia	History of Science	Watercolors
11	Conquistadors	Baltic States	Igneous Rocks	Creative Kids
12	Settlers	Peru & Bolivia	Sedimentary Rocks	Native American Art
13	13 Colonies	Central America	Metamorphic Rocks	Settler Sayings
14	Slave Trade	Brazil	Gems & Minerals	Colonial Art
15	The South Pacific	Australasia	Fossils	Principles of Art
16	The British in India	India	Chemical Reactions	Classical Music
17	Boston Tea Party	Japan	Reversible Reactions	Folk Music
18	Founding Fathers	Iran	Compounds & Solutions	Rococo
19	Declaring Independence	Samoa and Tonga	Oxidation & Reduction	Creative Crafts I
20	The American Revolution	South Africa	Acids & Bases	Creative Crafts II

4	History	Geography	Science	The Arts
1	American Government	USA	Heat & Temperature	Patriotic Music
2	Expanding Nation	Pacific States	Motors & Engines	Tall Tales
3	Industrial Revolution	U.S. Landscapes	Energy	Romantic Art I
4	Revolutions	Mountain West States	Energy Sources	Romantic Art II
5	Africa	U.S. Political Maps	Energy Conversion	Impressionism I
6	The West	Southwest States	Earth Structure	Impressionism II
7	Civil War	National Parks	Plate Tectonics	Post-Impressionism
8	World War I	Plains States	Earthquakes	Expressionism
9	Totalitarianism	U.S. Economics	Volcanoes	Abstract Art
10	Great Depression	Heartland States	Mountain Building	Kinds of Art
11	World War II	Symbols and Landmarks	Chemistry of Air & Water	War Art
12	Modern East Asia	The South States	Food Chemistry	Modern Art
13	India's Independence	People of America	Industry	Pop Art
14	Israel	Appalachian States	Chemistry of Farming	Modern Music
15	Cold War	U.S. Territories	Chemistry of Medicine	Free Verse
16	Vietnam War	Atlantic States	Food Chains	Photography
17	Latin America	New England States	Animal Groups	Latin American Art
18	Civil Rights	Home State Study	Instincts	Theater & Film
19	Technology	Home State Study II	Habitats	Architecture
20	Terrorism	America in Review	Conservation	Creative Kids

Unit 2-5

Printable Pack

This unit includes printables at the end. To make life easier for you we also created digital printable packs for each unit. To retrieve your printable pack for Unit 2-5, please visit

www.layers-of-learning.com/digital-printable-packs/

Put the printable pack in your shopping cart and use this coupon code:

1776UNIT2-5

Your printable pack will be free.

LAYERS OF LEARNING INTRODUCTION

This is part of a series of units in the Layers of Learning homeschool curriculum, including the subjects of history, geography, science, and the arts. Children from 1st through 12th can participate in the same curriculum at the same time – family school style.

The units are intended to be used in order as the basis of a complete curriculum (once you add in a systematic math, reading, and writing program). You begin with Year 1 Unit 1 no matter what ages your children are. Spend about 2 weeks on each unit. You pick and choose the activities within the unit that appeal to you and read the books from the book list that are available to you or find others on the same topic from your library. We highly recommend that you use the timeline in every history section as the backbone. Then flesh out your learning with reading and activities that highlight the topics you think are the most important.

Alternatively, you can use the units as activity ideas to supplement another curriculum in any order you wish. You can still use them with all ages of children at the same time.

When you've finished with Year One, move on to Year Two, Year Three, and Year Four. Then begin again with Year One and work your way through the years again. Now your children will be older, reading more involved books, and writing more in depth. When you have completed the sequence for the second time, you start again on it for the third and final time. If your student began with Layers of Learning in 1st grade and stayed with it all the way through she would go through the four year rotation three times, firmly cementing the information in her mind in ever increasing depth. At each level you should expect increasing amounts of outside reading and writing. High schoolers in particular should be reading extensively, and if possible, participating in discussion groups.

😊 😊 😊 These icons will guide you in spotting activities and books that are appropriate for the age of child you are working with. But if you think an activity is too juvenile or too difficult for your kids, adjust accordingly. The icons are not there as rules, just guides.

😊 GRADES 1-4

😊 GRADES 5-8

😊 GRADES 9-12

Within each unit we share:
- EXPLORATIONS, activities relating to the topic;
- EXPERIMENTS, usually associated with science topics;
- EXPEDITIONS, field trips;
- EXPLANATIONS, teacher helps or educational philosophies.

In the sidebars we also include Additional Layers, Famous Folks, Fabulous Facts, On the Web, and other extra related topics that can take you off on tangents, exploring the world and your interests with a bit more freedom. The curriculum will always be there to pull you back on track when you're ready.

You can learn more about how to use this curriculum at www.layers-of-learning.com/layers-of-learning-program/

UNIT THREE
ANGLO SAXONS – BRITAIN – WILD WEATHER – KING ARTHUR TALES

Freedom is a possession of inestimable value.
-Cicero, Roman Statesman

	LIBRARY LIST:
HISTORY	Search for: Anglo-Saxons, Augustine, Beowulf, Alfred the Great, Edward the Confessor

Search for: Anglo-Saxons, Augustine, Beowulf, Alfred the Great, Edward the Confessor

☺ <u>Beowulf and the Dragon</u> retold by Tessa Potter.

☺ <u>Anglo Saxons</u> by William Webb.

☺ <u>Beginning History: Saxon Villages</u> by Robin Place.

☺ ☻ <u>King Alfred: England's Greatest King</u> by Christina Dugan.

☺ ☻ <u>Who In The World Was the Unready King?</u> by Connie Clark. Biography of Ethelred the Unready, an easy reader.

☺ ☻ <u>Favorite Medieval Tales</u> by Mary Pope Osborne and Troy Howell. Contains a re-telling of Beowulf, The Sword in the Stone, Sir Gawain and the Green Knight, plus six others that you can read with your kids throughout this year's medieval history units.

☺ ☻ <u>Anglo Saxons</u> by John Reeve. An activity book from the British Museum.

☻ <u>When Augustine Came to Kent</u> by Barbara Willard. Historical novel. A young boy witnesses the historic meeting of St. Augustine and a Saxon King.

☻ <u>The Silver King: Edward the Confessor</u> by Margaret Stanley-Wrench. A biography written in 1966 about the last Anglo-Saxon king. Out of print, look for used copies or at your library.

☻ <u>The Timetraveler's Guide to Saxon and Viking London</u> by Joshua Doder. Looks at the archeology of London from this time period. Illustrated and fun!

☻ <u>Anglo-Saxons and Vikings</u> by Hazel Maskel and Abigail Wheatly. From Usborne.

☻ ☻ <u>The Shining Company</u> by Rosemary Sutcliff. Historical novel. Britons hopelessly defend their lands against the Saxon invaders. Brilliantly and movingly written.

☻ ☻ <u>The Eagle of the Ninth</u> by Rosemary Sutcliff. The first in a series of three historical novels about Roman legions as the Romans pull out of Britain and as the Anglo-Saxon invasions begin.

☻ ☻ <u>The King's Shadow</u> by Elizabeth Alder. A young Welsh boy thinks his life is over when his father is killed, his tongue is cut out, and he is sold as a slave, but then he gains the notice of Harold of Wessex. Historical novel that takes place just before and during the Norman invasion.

☻ ☻ <u>Beowulf</u> By Gareth Hinds. Graphic novel version for comic book lovers.

☻ ☻ <u>Beowulf Dragonslayer</u> by Rosemary Sutcliff. A translation especially for kids.

☻ <u>The Anglo-Saxons</u> by James Campbell, Eric John, and Patrick Wormald. Scholarly, but accessible, often used as a text book in colleges.

☻ <u>Beowulf</u>. Choose the Seamus Heaney translation. Beowulf should be an exciting hero tale, not a chore, and Heaney makes it both epic and accessible.

GEOGRAPHY

Search for: Great Britain, England, Scotland, Wales, British Isles, London, Edinburgh

☺ B is For Big Ben by Pamela Duncan Edwards.

☺ Katie in London by James Mayhew.

☺ The Great Smelly, Slobbery, Small-Tooth Dog: A Folktale from Great Britain by Margaret Read MacDonald.

☺ ☻ The Story of Scotland by Richard Brassey and Stewart Ross. A history in comic book style. It's written for younger kids, but don't be surprised if your teen sneaks it off.

☺ ☻ Royal Family of Britain Paper Dolls by Tom Tierney.

☺ ☻ This is Britain by Miroslav Sasek.

☺ ☻ This Is London by Miroslav Sasek.

☻ ☻ Britain and Ireland: A Visual Tour of the Enchanted Isles by Robin Currie.

☻ ☻ The Most Beautiful Villages in England by James Bentley. A photographic book.

☻ Watching the English: The Hidden Rules of English Behaviour by Kate Fox. An English anthropologist studies her own people and writes a tongue in cheek commentary on her findings . . . you may be surprised!

SCIENCE

Search for: storms

☺ ☻ ☻ Nature's Fury DVD from National Geographic. Great family viewing for all ages.

☺ It's Stormy by Julie Richards.

☺ The Magic School Bus Inside a Hurricane by Joanna Cole. Absolutely fabulous and packed with information as all Magic School Bus books are. Perfect for grade schoolers.

☺ Wild Weather by Katherine Kenah. An easy reader.

☺ ☻ Bill Nye the Science Guy: Storms DVD.

☺ ☻ Storms by Simon Seymour.

☻ Why Does Lightning Strike? By Terry Martin. Answers questions kids have about the weather.

☻ The Perfect Storm by Sebastian Junger. Real life events made into a journalistic novel. Takes you through the October 1991 storm that took the lives of six fishermen in the Atlantic. Delves into meteorology and the fishing industry on the way.

THE ARTS

Search for: King Arthur

☺ ☻ ☻ King Arthur and His Knights retold by Jim Weiss. Audio CD.

☺ The Kitchen Knight: A Tale of King Arthur by Margaret Hodges.

☺ ☻ King Arthur and His Knights of the Round Table by Roger Lancelyn Green.

☻ The Story of King Arthur and His Knights by Howard Pyle. Good readers at a younger age will enjoy it as well and younger kids would like it read aloud. Choose the unabridged version from Dover Publishers.

☻ King Arthur: Tales From the Round Table by Andrew Lang.

☻ Tales of King Arthur by Felicity Brooks.

☻ ☻ The Once and Future King by T.H. White.

☻ The King Arthur and His Knights by Sir Thomas Malory and Eugene Vinaver, ed.

☻ The King Arthur Trilogy by Rosemary Sutcliff.

HISTORY: ANGLO SAXONS

On the Web
Go to http://www.bbc.co.uk/schools/primaryhistory/anglo_saxons/ from the BBC to learn more about the Anglo Saxons.

Then, try this site with tons of information and pictures: http://cd7.e2bn.net/e2bn/leas/c99/schools/cd7/website/Anglo-Saxons.htm.

And finally, visit www.regia.org for more detailed information about these people and this period.

Fabulous Fact
Between the Roman abandonment of Britain and the Norman invasion, the Anglo Saxon people who established themselves in the British Isles kept a history of the region in a collection of manuscripts called the Anglo-Saxon Chronicle. It was written by monks at various monasteries all over Britain. It is the source for almost all the history we know of these people.

Fabulous Fact
The Saxons ruled themselves through the Witenagemot system. Learn more.

As the Romans pulled out of Britain, barbarian tribes poured in. The Angles, Saxons, and Jutes came from Denmark and northern Germany. It was not a peaceful invasion and though the British resisted, they were eventually slaughtered and pushed into Wales. The newcomers became known as the Anglo-Saxons and the land came to be called Angle-land, later evolving into England.

The Angles set up seven kingdoms and spent their idle summer months fighting wars with each other and squabbling about religion.

A reenactor wearing replicas of grave goods found at the Sutton-Hoo archeological site. Photo by Ziko-C and shared under CC license.

Within a few hundred years the invaders themselves were invaded, by the Danes this time. The Danes conquered all the Anglo kingdoms except Wessex, which was ruled by King Alfred. Alfred drove the Danes back. King Alfred made a treaty with the Danes, dividing the land. The Danish lands became known as the Danelaw and Alfred ruled the rest of Anglia. The Danes weren't finished yet though. They invaded Alfred's grandson's land and ruled for thirty years before being driven out by the Angles again.

Yet again, someone else wanted England. In order to get it he was willing to connive, scheme, and lay waste. His name was

William of Normandy. He was a Viking from northern France, who was supposedly under the authority of the French King, but who, in fact, ruled alone as a duke in his land. He had made verbal agreements with Edward the Confessor to take the crown when Edward, who was heir-less, died, though Edward had no legal authority to make such promises. The English king was elected by the Witan, he did not rule by divine right. William invaded England when the English Witan refused to elect him king. The lawfully elected king, Harold, was defeated after fending off simultaneous invasions from first Harold Hardrada of Norway and then William of Normandy. From this time the Normans became the ruling class, and the Saxons became subjects ruled over with an iron fist and no longer retaining their ancient freedoms.

☺ ☺ ☺ EXPLORATION: Timeline of Anglo-Saxons

Printable timeline squares are at the end of this unit.

- 400 AD Vortigern of Britain asked for Saxon help in conquering the Picts.
- 410-520 AD Angles, Saxons, and Jutes invaded and settled Britain, destroying the Christian religion wherever they settled.
- Early 500's King Arthur united his people in defense of their lands from the invaders. He was successful for a time.
- 597 AD Roman Christianity re-introduced by St. Augustine.
- 600 AD Britain divided into seven kingdoms.
- 663 AD Synod of Whitby decided to accept Roman Christianity over Celtic Christianity.
- 716 AD Mercian Kingdom dominated the rest of the Saxon Kingdoms south of the Humber River.
- 757 AD Offa, powerful Mercian King ruled.
- 867-874 AD The first Danish Viking invasion.
- 871-899 AD Alfred was elected King of Wessex, he and his daughter hold back the Danish Vikings.
- 924-939 AD Athelstan was King of England
- 1013-1042 AD Danes ruled England
- 1024-1066 AD Edward the Confessor was elected King of England
- 1066 AD William of Normandy (of Viking descent) conquered England.

☺ ☺ ☺ EXPLORATION: Anglo-Saxon Kingdoms Map

Use the Anglo-Saxon Kingdoms map from the end of this unit. Color each of these Anglo-Saxon kingdoms: Mercia, Northumbria, Kent, Wessex, East Anglia, and Essex. Also color the Pictish and Celtic kingdoms. The borders of these kingdoms

Famous Folks

Lady Godiva was an Anglo-Saxon noblewoman and the wife of Leofric, Earl of Mercia.

According to legend her husband had imposed harsh taxes on the people. Lady Godiva, seeing their suffering pleaded with her husband that he remit them or lighten them. He refused, but after repeated pleading he told her that if she would ride through the town of Coventry naked he would relieve all the tax burden. After ordering all the inhabitants inside and the windows shuttered she did ride through the town naked and her husband did remit the taxes.

Famous Folks

King Alfred is the only English king ever given the appellation "Great." Learn more about this amazing monarch.

Photo by Odejea, CC license

Fabulous Fact

The *Y Goddodin* is an old British poem about the men of Goddodin, a British post-Roman people who lived in northeast England; 360 warriors who died defending their homes from the Saxon invaders in a hopeless, but heroic, battle. The battle of these men was retold brilliantly by Rosemary Sutcliff in her novel, *The Shining Company*. Older kids can read the translated poem: http://www.maryjones.us/ctexts/a01a.html

changed rapidly as they fought one another almost constantly. Label King Otha's Dike and color it in brown. King Otha was the strongest of the Mercian kings and he built a guarded wall, or dike, to contain the depredations of the Welsh. The Welsh are the original Celtic inhabitants of the isles, who have been pushed to the far west by the Anglo-Saxons.

For the second map use "During the Danelaw." This time we'll show the land a few hundred years later in 886 AD. The Danes have invaded and a treaty has been made with them that they will have half the land, the Danelaw, and the Anglo-Saxons will retain their kingdom, Wessex, in the west. The Danelaw was part of the Kingdom of Cnut the great who also ruled part of Norway and all of Denmark. The Celtic (Wales and Strathclyde) and Pictish kingdoms are still there as well. In a few more years the English will drive the Danes out, but then England will be invaded and defeated by William of Normandy.

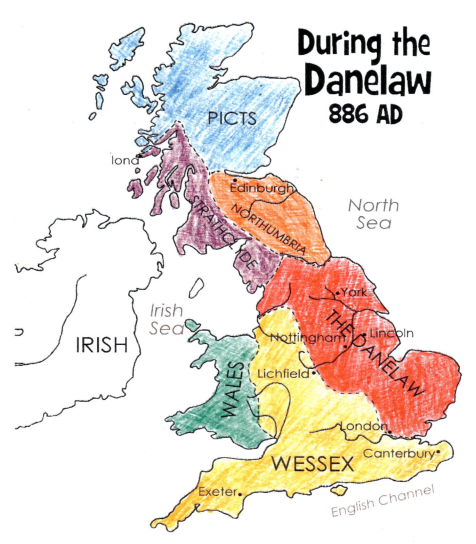

During the Danelaw 886 AD

PICTS

Iona

Edinburgh

North Sea

STRATHCLYDE

NORTHUMBRIA

Irish Sea

York

THE DANELAW

Nottingham • Lincoln

IRISH

WALES

Lichfield

London

Canterbury •

WESSEX

Exeter •

English Channel

Additional Layer

Divorce was very rare in Anglo-Saxon times and children and women were valued and protected by the law . . . a very rare state of affairs in the world.

Additional Layer

If you were a free man or woman you proved it by wearing a seax knife everywhere you went. Slaves were not allowed weapons.

Additional Layer

Famous Men of the Middle Ages by John A. Haaren is an illustrated collection of thirty-five short biographies of men (plus Joan of Arc) from the medieval period in Europe. Read it aloud with your kids.

Our Island Story by H.E. Marshall is a history of England for children from ancient times up to the death of Queen Victoria. Read it aloud with your kids. The Phoenix Press Edition has full-color photos, which are well worth it.

Look for the sequel, *This Country of Ours*, by the same author about America from settlement to 1912.

😊 😊 **EXPLORATION: Old English**

The Saxons spoke a language that today we call Old English. Since they were from Germany, it was a form of German. English is called a Germanic language because of these roots, though English also is heavily rooted in Latin and has great influences from the Scandinavian Vikings and the Norman French.

Though most people couldn't read and write at the time, those who did used runes at first. Over time the Anglo-Saxons changed to using the Latin alphabet, but that was after they were converted to Christianity and Latin was the language of the learned and the church.

Here are the runes used by the Anglo-Saxons. Each symbol has a name and a phonetic sound associated with it. The first rune is

Explanation

Today a neighbor stopped by and asked, "Are your kids just VORACIOUS readers?" I hated my answer. No. Oh, how I wish they were. I wish I had a magic switch to turn on that made them love books. Don't get me wrong – they love stories. They love having me read to them. We've read since they were, well, in utero. But my kids still have to be ~~forced~~ told to pick up a book.

It makes me feel like quite a failure to tell you this. But I still want to tell you, because often when I've felt like a failure at something I meet someone who has the same struggles. I meet someone who is searching for the same answers I am, and then I feel like maybe I'm not all alone.

I really hope someday I can amend this with a disclaimer at the bottom saying, "Keep reading to your kids! It took a long time, but eventually my kids fell in love with books!" The truth is, I'm not sure it will ever happen, but we will read.

Karen

named feoh, which means "wealth" in Anglo-Saxon and has the phonetic sound "f." Most of them have equivalent phonetic symbols in English, but a few do not. The third rune has the phonetic sound of "th" in English. The eighth rune which looks similar to a P has the phonetic sound "w." The fourth rune on the third row makes a "ng" sound like in "sing." The seventh rune on the last row makes the sound "cw." Try some runes out by writing your name or a short sentence in runes.

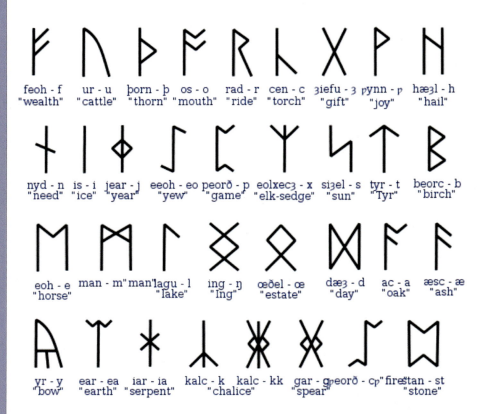

When the great King Alfred reigned he had many Latin church texts and poems of his people translated into his language, Wessex Anglo-Saxon, or old English. Here is an excerpt from Beowulf, first in Old English, with the modern English literal translation below it so you can compare. Old English was written down phonetically, so you can get a good idea of what the words sounded like by sounding them out, though we probably pronounce some things differently to what they did.

> Hwaet! We Gar-Dena in gear-dagnum,
> What! We of Spear-Danes in yore-days,
>
> beod-cyninga, brym gefruon,
> of nation-kings, did glory learn about,

hu oa aebelingas ellen fremedon
how those noblemen did courage promote.

Oft Scyld Scefing sceabena breatum,
Oft did Scyld Scefing scatter threats,

monegum maebum, meodosetha ofteah,
of many clans of mead-settlements deprive,

egsode eorlas. Syooan aerest wearo.
and terrify earls. Since first he became.

☺ ☻ ☻ EXPLORATION: Beowulf

Beowulf is a very old bardic poem written by an Anglo-Saxon minstrel. It is the only complete epic poem from these days to survive to the present. It was written down at some point, while most others never were. Minstrels composed and memorized their poems completely in their own heads, then if the poem was good enough, other minstrels would also memorize it and they would pass it down as well.

Beowulf fighting the dragon.
Art by J.R. Skelton

Though Beowulf was written in England by an Anglo Saxon, it was set in Sweden. A monster is terrorizing a local king's hall, but no one is brave enough to take on the monster so Beowulf comes from across the sea in Denmark to challenge the monster . . . read the tale to find out what happens.

Even though the poem takes place in Sweden, it tells of Anglo-Saxon customs that the composer would have been familiar with. Read some of these passages here:

http://www.earlybritishkingdoms.com/kids/beowulf_quotes.html

Draw a picture of one of the Anglo-Saxon items described in the poem.   We'll carry on with Beowulf in the next unit as well, including more activities in the arts section of 3-6.

Writer's Workshop

No one knows anything at all about the author of Beowulf, not even a name. Write your own bio of this author from your imagination. Give him or her an Anglo-Saxon name and tell which village they were from and how they got their training as a bard. You may need to do a bit of research about Anglo Saxon bards. Then put it all down in your Writer's Notebook.

Explanation

We tend to think of the "classics" as dry and boring, but the truth is only the best of the best has been preserved down through the ages. If you're reading a bad or dated translation though, you're sunk. We try really hard to find the best translations or re-tellings of the old classics and give you our top recommendations. Pick a translation or even a simplified re-telling of Beowulf that you actually enjoy reading, because that's kind of the point. The bard would be horrified to think you were bored or didn't "get it." This stuff is definitely supposed to be popular level material, not for highbrows.

Fabulous Fact

Anglo-Saxons often invaded the Roman cities and took them over, but they weren't so interested in the buildings, just the city walls. They knew the walls could provide good protection.

They built their own huts and wooden homes with thatched roofs inside the city walls the Romans had built. The homes were built in little groups that surrounded a larger hall.

Additional Layer

The military was organized under earls, who had a body of permanent troops called housecarls. In addition to these professional soldiers, the king or an earl or thane could raise the fyrd, a militia body made up of citizen soldiers. All adult men were under obligation to defend the land against invaders and bandits. But the fyrd were free men and could only be legally called up for a short time.

☺ ☻ EXPLORATION: Society

Most Anglo-Saxons lived on farm estates of great lords or on their own personal farms. There were small towns as well, but they weren't important or influential.

Over time the greatest of the chieftains rose to become royalty. At first there were many kingdoms and each king was equal to another, but eventually the power consolidated into the hands of one family, the royalty of Wessex. The king was always chosen from among this family (which includes cousins, uncles, grandparents, great uncles, second cousins and so forth) but the position of king did not always move from a father to his direct descendant. The king was chosen by a vote in a council called the witan. The witan was made up of eoldermen (or elder men).

Eoldermen were the nobility. This class also included the high ranking church officials. The position of eolderman was not hereditary either, but was appointed by the king for life. It was a job where the noble was responsible for the well being of the people of his shire and also for their defense in case of attack. The eolderman also had obligations he must perform to the king, including collecting taxes and raising armies in time of war.

Serving the eoldermen were the thanes who were the military class. Thanes often owned land as well, within their eolderman's lands or sometimes directly from the king. Lower ranking church men and women also belonged to this class.

Royal Family
↓
Eoldermen
(nobility)
↓
Thanes
(Military class)
↓
Churls
(Freemen farmers)
↓
Slaves

Churls were the freemen farmers. They were allowed to bear arms and were expected to serve in the fyrd, or army, when called upon. They also served on community councils or moots. They lived on their eolderman's lands and owned their own piece, which they either paid rent for or owned outright, depending on their condition. Some churls were servants of their lords, owning no land of their own, but in return the lord cared for their well-being. The terms of their relationship were set forth by law.

Finally, there were slaves. Their treatment was also set forth by law, including the food, shelter, housing, and human rights they could expect. They were allowed to own property and make extra money in their spare time. It was possible for them to buy their freedom. Slaves were not allowed to bear arms, marry, travel, or leave their lord's land without permission. In addition, they did not receive the same protection of the law as freemen.

Make finger puppets of each of these classes. Make a copy of the puppets from the end of this unit, color the figures, and cut them out. The holes at the bottom should be cut out as well and then your fingers go through the holes to make the "legs" of the figure.

☺ ☺ EXPLORATION: Specialization

Many of the Anglo-Saxons were farmers. They plowed, planted crops, and cared for animals. Some had special skills and did specific jobs though. Blacksmiths made tools and weapons, woodworkers made furniture and carts, potters made pottery and dishes, and jewelers created beautiful beads and jewelry.

Choose an item the Anglo-Saxons would have had. Make a flow chart showing what would have had to happen for them to get that product since they couldn't just head down to their local Wal-Mart to pick it up.

For example, a tunic didn't come from the store on a hanger. A sheep's wool would have to be gathered, cleaned, dyed, spun, woven into cloth, cut, and then hand-sewn. Phew! You've got a tunic.

Specialization certainly simplified things, but they still didn't enjoy the factory and machine style production we do today.

☺ ☺ EXPLORATION: Anglo-Saxon Women

When an Anglo-Saxon woman wed, she was presented with a contract from her husband that outlined all the gifts that he was giving to her. These included land, livestock, and slaves. This gave women independence and security in case something happened to her husband.

At home she probably wove cloth and helped with the cooking and children, though she likely had slaves to do these things alongside her. Her wealth and status dictated her position in society. The wealthier she was, the more freedom she enjoyed.

Fabulous Fact

We don't mention them much, but there was a third group who invaded at the same time as the Angles and Saxons. They are called the Jutes and they came from Denmark. They settled in the south of England.

Fabulous Fact

Anglo-Saxon England was more egalitarian than any society until modern times. Women were equal to their husbands, including the queen, who co-ruled as an equal with her husband. Women were independent and had great influence and power in public life as well as private. This changed with the 1066 invasion by William of Normandy who brought Norman customs which had been adopted from old Roman traditions, which we are heirs to today.

Additional Layer

Many stories have been told about King Arthur trying to defend his beloved homeland against the Anglo-Saxon invasion. Some people think King Arthur is a real historical figure and others think he is pure fiction. No one is sure. What do you think?

Women wore jewelry to show their status and importance. Brooches were commonly designed with animals, circles, swirls, and dots adorning them. They would've been worn at the top of a woman's cloak to fasten it. Design a brooch that includes all of these motifs in combination. Start by drawing a simple circle, then fill it in with all the themes. Some were pure silver or gold, but others were very colorful. Color your brooch.

☺ ☺ ☺ EXPLORATION: TIMBER!

Timber was the most important natural resource to the Anglo-Saxons. Their carpenters were probably really busy people because many of their possessions were crafted from wood, which was very plentiful in that area. Dishes, buildings, ships, musical instruments, bridges, coffins, weapons, furniture, barrels, game boards, toys, plows, wagons, carts, wheels – all were made of wood.

Compare the items of the Anglo-Saxons with the same items we have today. Make a list of the items and record the materials we commonly use today to make them.

☺ ☺ ☺ EXPLORATION: Riddles

Anglo-Saxons loved to be entertained. They gathered in the lord's hall to hear stories and listen to songs. Often the storytellers were also musicians and sang and played instruments in the middle of their stories. They also loved to tell riddles.

Can you guess these riddles:

I appear on the ground like a blanket and melt in the midday sun. What am I? {snow!}

Only one color, but not one size. Stuck at the bottom, yet easily flies. Present in sunshine, but not in rain. Doing no harm and feeling no pain. What am I? {a shadow}

No legs have I to dance. No lungs have I to breathe.
No life I have to live or die, And yet I do all three. What am I? {fire}

Come up with a few riddles of your own or find a riddle book for more fun.

☺ ☻ EXPLORATION: Lucky Charms

Anglo-Saxons were definitely superstitious. They believed in magic, potions, protection stones and jewelry, and lucky charms.

Take a survey. Ask 10 people you know if they have (or have ever had) a lucky charm. Do you have any lucky charms or superstitions? Have you ever wished on a star? Have you not washed your uniform because you won the big game? Do you ever wear a piece of jewelry for luck?

Here's a little rhyme you can memorize about lucky charms:

You can rub your lucky penny til it's smoother than a stone,
You can rub your lucky rabbit's foot down to the bone.
You can close your eyes and wish upon a star,
But you can't press your luck . . . too far!

☺ ☻ ☻ EXPLORATION: Anglo-Saxon Kings and Queens

Visit: http://www.royal.gov.uk/HistoryoftheMonarchy/Kingsan dQueensofEngland/TheAnglo-Saxonkings/Overview.aspx. It is an official history of the British Monarchy. Choose one of the Anglo-Saxon kings to learn more about and write a report on.

Younger kids may also be interested in the Anglo-Saxon coloring sheet from the end of this unit. Dragons, such as the one on the shield, were often a symbol of the Anglo-Saxons.

Additional Layer

Anglo-Saxons may not have been good sports. In their swimming races they were allowed to shove each other under the water! They loved ball games, and played one similar to street hockey. They also had weight lifting competitions using heavy rocks and enjoyed wrestling.

Fabulous Fact

Sutton Hoo ship burial, located in East Anglia, Britain, is one of the greatest finds ever.

Pottery, weapons, bodies, spoons, jewelry, silver bowls, harnesses, belts, clothing, and other household goods were found in the burial chamber. This helmet, reconstructed, is the most famous of all the finds.

Photo by Gernott Keller, CC license.

GEOGRAPHY: BRITAIN

Fabulous Fact

United Kingdom of Great Britain and Ireland is the official name of the country. Great Britain refers only to the largest island. England refers only to the kingdom of England in the southeast of the island. The United Kingdom consists of England, Scotland, Wales and Northern Ireland.

Additional Layer

Most of us are familiar with literature of the British Isles.

Here are a few we love:

Winnie the Pooh by A.A. Milne

Chronicles of Narnia by C.S. Lewis

Thomas the Tank Engine by Rev. Audrey

Pride and Prejudice by Jane Austen

Alice in Wonderland by Lewis Carroll

The Lord of the Rings by J.R.R. Tolkien

Harry Potter by J.K. Rowling

Five Children and It by Edith Nesbit

Peter Pan by J.M. Barrie

Great Britain is the name of the larger island and also the political unit which includes the former kingdoms of England, Wales, Scotland, and Northern Ireland. Officially it is called the United Kingdom of Great Britain and Northern Ireland. Many people also call it the UK. The islands were first inhabited by a people we know almost nothing about. The Celts soon invaded, but were then taken over by Romans. Then the Romans were invaded by the Anglo-Saxons who were conquered by the Danes, but the Danes were driven out again. Finally, the Anglo-Saxons were conquered by William of Normandy. The royalty of England today descends from William. England also conquered or united with the other kingdoms of the nearby isles, and today the country is known as Great Britain.

There are two main islands and thousands of small ones that make up the British Isles. The south and east of the island is covered with rolling hills, and the northern and western areas are more mountainous, especially in Wales and Scotland.

The British speak primarily English, though many people also speak Welsh, Scottish Gaelic, Scots, and Cornish. Their language and many of their customs have been spread throughout the world as a result of their colonialism from the Elizabethan Age to the Edwardian. Their example of law, limited kingship, free markets, and rights of man have also spread the world over and blessed mankind.

Their government is a constitutional monarchy, with a parliament and prime minister. The queen is largely a figurehead with little real power. Britain, besides ruling itself, has many protectorates and colonies, the largest of which is Canada.

☻ ☻ ☻ **EXPLORATION: Great Britain Map**
Label a map of Great Britain. You can find an outline map at the end of this unit. Use the index of a student atlas to look up the places below. Do as many or as few as you like.

Cities:

London	Kingston Upon Hull
Birmingham	Bristol
Leeds	Manchester
Glasgow	Edinburgh
Sheffield	Liverpool
Bradford	

Political Units

Wales	East Anglia
Northern Ireland	England
Scotland	

Rivers

Thames	Ribble
Mersey	Severn
Humber	Tees

Seas

English Channel	Firth of Lorn
North Sea	The Little Minch
Celtic Sea	The Minch
Irish Sea	Moray Firth
Atlantic Ocean	Firth of Forth
Bristol Channel	The Wash
Straits of Dover	

Islands and Land Features

Isle of Wight	Ben Nevis
Outer Hebrides	The Lake District
Inner Hebrides	The Fens
Land's End	The Pennines

☻ ☻ ☻ **EXPLORATION: Afternoon Tea**
In the U.S.A. tea is a drink; in the U.K. it's a meal. Traditional tea includes drinking tea, but not always.

Tea is the evening meal, but many people now just call it dinner or supper. A traditional evening meal consists of roast meat, potatoes, and another cooked vegetable. Though today the British eat foods from all over the world, just as Americans do.

Additional Layer

The English Robin is smaller and rounder than the North American Robin.

Famous Folks

One of the most iconic of British rock groups is the Beatles. Listen to some of their music.

Famous Folks

Winston Churchill was Prime Minister of Great Britain during WWII, brilliantly leading the country in its darkest days.

Additional Layer

Oxford University is the oldest university in the English-speaking world, having been founded sometime before 1096 AD. It is also one of the top universities in the world.

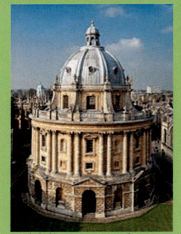

Radcliffe Camera Library at Oxford.
Photo by DAVID ILIFF.
License: CC-BY-SA 3.0

Additional Layer

At its height in 1922, the British Empire consisted of one quarter of all the land on Earth, the largest empire in history. That empire has had a huge effect on today's world, with the English language becoming the lingua franca of the business and science worlds. English law has also become the basis of many countries around the world. England gave the world prosperity, stability, and ultimately more freedom than any other land on Earth.

For this activity you'll have more fun if you have afternoon tea, which is a light meal served in the late afternoon. Break out your fine china and serve tea and crumpets, scones and jam. Oh, and don't forget to eat with your fork in the left hand and say please and thank you.

Crumpets
½ cup warm water
2 tsp. sugar
1 Tbsp. yeast
2 ½ cups flour
½ tsp. salt
1 ½ cups milk

Mix the warm water, sugar and yeast in a bowl and let stand for ten minutes. Mix in the rest of the ingredients and allow to stand for 30 minutes.

Heat up a griddle to medium low heat and grease it lightly. Set cookie cutters or canning rings onto the griddle and pour the batter in, allowing them to fry slowly. Turn after 10 minutes. Fry for another minute. Serve warm with butter and jam.

Scones
(Similar to American biscuits)
2 cups flour
1 Tbsp. baking powder
2 Tbsp. sugar
½ tsp. salt
3 Tbsp. butter
1 beaten egg
¾ cup milk

Mix the dry ingredients and cut in the butter. Add egg and milk and stir. Briefly knead dough on a floured surface, then cut into rounds with a biscuit cutter or upside down glass. Bake at 450° F for 15 minutes until golden. Serve with butter and jam.

☺ ☺ ☺ EXPLORATION: Compare 'Em

Compare the U.K. with your home state or country. Make a chart showing mottoes, flags, population, largest city, highest mountain, normal temperature ranges, longest river, largest lake, and population density.

☺ ☺ EXPLORATION: Union Jack

The flag of the United Kingdom is nicknamed the Union Jack.

It is a composite of the red cross of St. George, the patron saint of England; the white diagonal cross flag of Saint Andrew of Scotland; and the red diagonal cross of Saint Patrick from Ireland.

Use a pencil, ruler, scissors, and red, white, and blue construction paper and craft your own Union Jack.

☺ ☺ EXPLORATION: The King's English

Though both the United States and Britain speak English, many of our words and expressions are different. See if you can match the British word to an actual item. Gather these items, (or a picture or toy representing them): Delivery truck, underwear, athletic shoes, rain boots, diaper, pencil eraser, bath robe, school grades, parking lot, crossing guard, sidewalk, gasoline, closet, trash can, radio, french fries, cookies, bacon, dessert, soccer ball, flashlight.

Here are the British words to try to match up. Write them on index cards or pieces of paper. (They are in the same order as the American words above so you have the key.) Lorry, pants, trainers, wellingtons, nappy, rubber, dressing gown, marks, car park, lollipop man, pavement, petrol, wardrobe, bin, wireless, chips, biscuits, rasher, pudding, football, torch.

☺ ☺ ☺ EXPEDITION: UK

If you have the chance at all, you really should hop on a plane and make the U.K. your destination. If that's not a possibility, you can go to www.Destination360.com, a website with a plethora of travel information, and search for UK. You can click on as many of the destinations in the sidebar as you want. Each destination has a beautiful picture of the site and a description of what you will see there.

Additional Layer

Quintessential British sports include association football (soccer), cricket, rowing, and rugby.

To the north in Scotland you'll find the original home of a popular little game called golf.

Fabulous Fact

A bridge has spanned the River Thames, linking London with Southwark since the days of the Roman Legions. This is known as London Bridge, though the actual structure has been updated and replaced several times over the two millennium since it was first built. During medieval times the bridge was covered with buildings and even a church dedicated to the martyr, Thomas Becket, by the king who had him killed. Find out more about the history of London Bridge.

Medieval London Bridge, which stood for 600 years.

Politics

Britain has two major political parties: The Labour Party and the Conservative Party.

The Labour Party is for nationalization of certain industries, labor unions, welfare measures, multiculturalism, and other socialist measures.

The Conservative Party, also known as Tories, believe in free markets, traditional family values, close ties with the United States, and a strong military stance.

☻ EXPLORATION: London

London is a bustling city. It's the biggest city in the European Union with a population of about 12 million people.

Look up the populations of these other large cities and compare:

- New York
- Los Angeles
- Tokyo
- Paris
- Sydney
- Mexico City
- Sao Paulo
- Moscow
- Shanghai
- Cairo
- Hong Kong

Put the cities in order, biggest to smallest.

☺ ☻ EXPLORATION: May Day

May 1st is May Day! It's a festival that marks the coming of spring, and is a day of music, dancing, and flowers. The children, adorned in beautiful clothing and flowers, dance around a maypole. Kids prepare for the dance for months in advance, learning the steps. Each year a May Queen is chosen and given a flower crown. The kids all vote for the prettiest girl to become the May Queen.

During May Day it's popular to wear flowers on your head. The boys have straw hats with flowers and the girls wear hats or flower garlands. Make your own hat or garland. You can use artificial flowers or real ones. A wire hanger or a piece of 20 gauge wire is perfect for the base. Use floral tape to secure the leaves and flowers on to the wire base.

Famous Folks

William Shakespeare was a playwright and poet who lived in England during the reigns of Queen Elizabeth and King James. He is most famous for his plays like *Hamlet*, *Romeo and Juliet*, and *Macbeth*. In Unit 3-5 we'll spend a whole Arts section just on Shakespeare.

☺ ☺ ☻ EXPLORATION: Royal Residence

The British Royal family owns the biggest royal home in the entire world, Windsor Castle. It has been the main royal home since William the Conqueror (over a thousand years!). The royal family actually owns quite a few homes, many of which are inhabited by several families within the royal family.

Go see what Windsor Castle is like inside by exploring the virtual rooms of the castle at the official website of The British Monarchy: www.royal.gov/uk/TheRoyalResidences/WindsorCastle/VirtualRooms/Overview/aspx.

Write a story that takes place inside the castle, either historical or modern.

Fabulous Fact

One landmark of England is Stonehenge. This ancient circle of standing stones is located in Salisbury Plain.

You can learn more about Stonehenge and the ancient people who built it in Unit 1-3.

Memorization Station

http://youtu.be/W_Z5LpHuXVE

They're changing guard at
Buckingham Palace -
Christopher Robin went down
with Alice.
Alice is marrying one of the
guard.
"A soldier's life is terrible
hard," Says Alice.

They're changing guard at
Buckingham Palace -
Christopher Robin went down
with Alice.
We saw a guard in a sentry-
box.
"One of the sergeants looks
after their socks," Says Alice.

They're changing guard at
Buckingham Palace -
Christopher Robin went down
with Alice.
We looked for the King, but he
never came.
"Well, God take care of him,
all the same," Says Alice.

They're changing guard at
Buckingham Palace -
Christopher Robin went down
with Alice.
They've great big parties
inside the grounds.
"I wouldn't be King for a
hundred pounds," Says Alice.

They're changing guard at
Buckingham Palace -
Christopher Robin went down
with Alice.
A face looked out, but it wasn't
the King's.
"He's much too busy a-signing
things," Says Alice.

They're changing guard at
Buckingham Palace -
Christopher Robin went down
with Alice.
"Do you think the King knows
all about me?"
"Sure to, dear, but it's time for
tea," Says Alice.

EXPLORATION: Changing of the Guard

Go to You Tube and search for The Changing of the Guard. The Royal Channel has a really neat eight and a half minute video showing the changing of the guard.

http://youtu.be/kzctIZreoWQ

There is a commentary as well; it tells all about the significance of the changing of the guard.

Now stand as still as can be while someone tries to get you to laugh. It is said that no one can get the soldiers to laugh while on guard.

EXPLORATION: Royal Wedding

We still love to follow the lives of royalty, even if they have very little effect on policy-making and world politics. Much of the world tuned in to see the 2011 royal wedding of Prince William and Catherine Middleton.

http://youtu.be/p7JIBkPNCcU

Go to You Tube and watch a bit of it, then write a paragraph explaining why you believe the world is so fascinated with the royals, and in particular, British Royals. Include your opinion of this fascination.

EXPLORATION: Big Ben

Big Ben is not the name of the famous building, just the bell inside the tower. The whole building is called the Elizabeth Tower and the giant clock is called the Great Clock. Color the picture of this famous landmark, which you will find at the end of this unit. You can take a tour of the tower at:

http://www.parliament.uk/bigben

SCIENCE: WILD WEATHER

Severe weather: hail, blizzards, high winds, thunder and lightning, freezing rain, wildfires, hurricanes, tornadoes, tidal waves, and other natural disasters probably have been and most likely will be a part of your life.

Storms are created when banks of air with contrasting pressures, high vs. low, butt up against one another. Swirling fronts of air create wind and thunderheads. In some cases they can also create hurricanes and tornadoes. All that moving air creates a lot of friction, often resulting in crackling lighting storms which can lead to wildfires.

Storms can cause a lot of destruction with high winds ripping roofs off buildings, sending objects flying into structures, leveling crops, destroying trees, bringing down power lines, causing storm surges that flood coastal towns, or dumping so much precipitation that river side towns are flooded. Winter storms can grow dangerously cold with wind whipping heat from buildings, and felling trees which are laden with heavy falls of snow. The falling trees often take out power lines or damage homes and businesses. Heavy snow can collapse the roofs of buildings and keep people stranded at home for days on end.

☺ ☺ EXPERIMENT: Thunder

Thunder is produced when lightning creates heat which causes the air to expand very quickly. The fast expansion causes thunder. You can make a mini thunder boom.

Fabulous Fact
A single cumulonimbus cloud can hold about as much water as 2000 Olympic-sized swimming pools.

Fabulous Fact
A forest ranger named Roy Sullivan was known as the human lightning rod. Before he died in 1983 he'd been struck by lightning seven times!

Additional Layer
Learn the safety tips to follow for a lightning storm. If you live in a hurricane or tornado zone, learn how to stay safe in those storms too.

Here is a PDF from the National Weather Service which teaches how storms are formed, how serious the damage can be, and how to keep your family and structures safe in a storm.

http://www.nws.noaa.gov/om/severeweather/resources/ttl6-10.pdf

Emergency Plan

In case of an emergency here are some essentials you should have in your house: candles, flashlights with batteries, blankets, 72 hour kit of food, emergency water, radio with batteries, and a meeting place in case family members are separated.

Keep all your items together so you can grab them quickly in case you have to evacuate from a hurricane, wildfire, or flood.

Also have a plan for how to spend your time if you are stranded at home for hours on end, especially if the power is out. Keeping up morale can be just as important as keeping warm in an emergency situation.

Have game boards, cards, books to read aloud, or let your kids do a talent show.

Additional Layer

Forest or grass fires are often caused by lightning storms. Find out more about this and determine the strategy you would follow if you were given the task of managing a forest.

How has wild fire management changed over the last decades?

You need a brown paper lunch sack. Blow it up and trap the air inside then smack the bottom of the sack hard with your hand. You'll make it explode and create a loud pop. It's the same principle that makes thunder boom.

☻ EXPLORATION: How Far Away Is it?

During a thunderstorm you can quickly and easily tell how far away the storm is. Watch for a flash of lightning. The second you see a flash, start your stopwatch. When you hear the thunder, stop the stopwatch. For every five seconds the storm is one mile away.

Fill in this chart:

5 seconds	1 mile
10 seconds	
15 seconds	
20 seconds	

If the storm is 15 miles away or more, you will never hear the thunder at all.

☺ ☻ EXPERIMENT: Lightning

Lightning occurs when violent winds high in the sky cause ice particles to move rapidly back and forth, rubbing against one another. All this movement creates static electricity. Eventually the static electricity becomes so great that it must be discharged.

The lightning will streak across the sky, dispersing the electricity and sending it into the ground, sometimes hitting objects on the ground first.

Think of it like your clothes dryer. If you fail to put a dryer sheet in, the action of the clothes turning around and around over and over builds up a lot of static electricity and you sure notice it when you try to wear those clothes. Exactly the same thing happens in the clouds.

You can make miniature lightning. Put on socks, natural fibers work best, and scuffle your feet across a carpet, again natural fibers work best. Now touch a metal doorknob. A spark of electricity will arc between your finger and the metal, giving you a little shock. You can also do this by rubbing a balloon on your hair.

😊 😊 😊 EXPLORATION: Hurricanes Brewing

To learn more about hurricanes visit www.nohc.noaa.gov. You can see any current storms brewing, learn about hurricane preparedness, and if you type "kids" into their search box, links to interactive activities on the web will appear, such as making your own hurricane. From the homepage there is a link

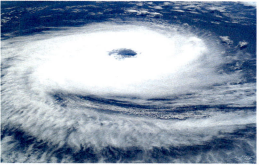

Fabulous Fact
In Australia they call hurricanes "Willy Willies."

Fabulous Fact
Sometimes we call tornadoes twisters because they spin.

Additional Layer

The amount of damage and disruption a storm causes often depends a great deal on the preparation of the people. Well developed nations rarely experience loss of life even close to that experienced by third world countries in similar disasters. Closer to home, we in the northern Rockies laugh when people in Seattle freak out over a few inches of snow. But we're used to it and have the proper equipment to deal with the problem. The same is true on a larger scale.

What can be done to help these unprepared countries?

Two basic approaches are tried: 1. Give them money and resources to aid the problem. 2. Work for more freedom so they can be prosperous and help themselves.

What do you think?

Tell some weather jokes. Here a few corny ones to get you started. Then you can make up some of your own.

What did the tornado say to the other tornado? *Let's twist again like we did last summer.* (I told that one to my kids and nobody laughed. Maybe it was my delivery?)

What did the hurricane say to the meteorologist? *I've got my eye on you.*

How many tornadoes does it take to screw in a light bulb? *One, it just twists and twists and twists.*

What happened when the cow was lifted up by the Twister? *Udder disaster.*

What kind of precipitation do pro football clouds throw down? *Hail Mary's.*

What is the most solemn type of cloud? *Cirrus (serious).*

When two hurricanes formed off the coast, what did the meteorologist say? *Two eyes are better than one.* (I warned you at the beginning that they were corny).

How does a hurricane see? *With one eye.*

What is a king's favorite type of precipitation? *Hail.*

to "blank tracking charts" which you can print out and use to track the storm yourself.

☺ ☻ EXPLORATION: Hurricane Names
Hurricanes are named using people's names. They alternate boy, girl throughout the season. Do a little research to find out if a hurricane was ever named after you. In 2001 there were hurricanes Michelle and Karen in the same year {that's us!}. Cool.

EXPLANATION: Tornadoes
Tornadoes are tall funnel clouds. They form when an updraft of warm, moist air rises up through a thunderstorm. The updraft rises and starts to rotate. They always form over land.

The winds in a tornado spiral around a narrow eye (where the air is calm right in the middle). The winds are so strong they can pick up cars, trees, and even houses!

Tornadoes die when they travel over colder ground or when clouds above them break up the winds.

☺ ☻ EXPERIMENT: Eye of the Tornado
Try dumping water out of a water bottle first by merely turning it upside down, then by giving it a swirl first.

The swirling water empties from the bottle much more quickly than the water that is dumped out.

The center of the swirling water is empty air, which allows air to move up inside

the water bottle and fix the pressure differences you create when you dump out the water. Tornadoes in nature have a center of "empty" air too, a place where the air isn't swirling. The air is moving though, it is moving up. Compare the motion to your water bottle. What effect will the upward moving air in the center have on the weather of a tornado?

☺ ☻ EXPLORATION: Tornado Tube
This version of the tornado in a bottle is impressive. You'll need 2 large plastic pop bottles, duct tape, water, and food coloring (optional).

Fill one of the bottles with water and then securely tape the two mouths of the bottles together so they won't leak.

If you tip it over the water will take a long time to go from one bottle to the other. But if you give it a good circular swirl the water will go down quickly in a swirling, tornado-style way.

As the water gets moving quickly it pushes out against the bottle and leaves a little hole in the middle (the eye of the storm). The hole lets air release from the bottom bottle to the top one, leaving space for the water to descend.

Additional Layer

The Dust Bowl drought was probably the worst drought in the history of America to date. Read *Children of the Dust Bowl* by Jerry Stanley to learn the whole story.

Fabulous Fact

Which direction do hurricanes and tornadoes turn?

Did you know it is the same direction in the northern hemisphere always? It is the opposite direction in the southern hemisphere. What happens if they cross the equator? Why?

Northern hemisphere storm

Southern hemisphere storm

This same phenomenon happens in a real tornado, except it's happening to air, not water. Technically, this tornado in a bottle should be called a whirlpool, not a tornado.

☺ ☺ **EXPLORATION: Storm Chasers**

Go to www.dsc.discovery.com/tv/storm-chasers to see an episode of *Storm Chasers*. Watch weather enthusiasts in action as they chase down wild storms.

☺ ☺ ☺ **EXPLORATION: Floods**

Floods are the most frequent weather disaster. Floods can happen several ways:

- River floods happen when it rains so much that a river overflows its banks.
- Snowmelts happen much the same way river floods do, except that instead of the excess water coming from rain, it comes from quickly melting snow from nearby mountains.
- Flash floods usually have little warning. When a storm drops a lot of rain in a short time in one specific area it can flood streets, houses, and anything in its path.
- Sea floods happen on the coast. Strong winds on the coast create waves and swells so big they can wash into the shore and create flooding.

Divide a sheet of paper into four parts and draw each of these kinds of floods. Label the flood types and put it in your science notebook. Check the news to see if floods have happened recently anywhere in the world. Which kind of flood was it?

😊 😊 EXPLORATION: Drought

Droughts are the deadliest of all natural disasters. We often don't think of them like that because the horror is spread out over long periods of time, and sometimes hardly even makes the news. Without rain, crops die, and people starve during times of famine. Animals also starve and die from lack of drinking water.

Many places in the world now have water restrictions put in place by their governments in order to try to prevent droughts. Research in the news to see if there are any droughts in the world right now . . . I bet there are even if it doesn't make the national headlines. Write an opinion essay on whether or not you think governments should control natural resources like water. Why?

😊 😊 EXPLANATION: Blizzards

Blizzards are severe snowstorms. It's only a blizzard if the wind is blowing at least 30 miles per hour. It also has to last at least 3 hours or it doesn't count.

They are created when a mass of warm air and a mass of cold air collide really quickly. The two fronts meeting cause strong winds and storm clouds, which, if it's cold enough, means lots of snow. The winds make the snow an even bigger problem because they blow snow around from the ground too.

The biggest problems with blizzards are that they often cause blackouts (not good when it's that cold outside!), make buildings collapse from the weight of the snow, and make transportation impossible because of the deep snow and bad visibility.

Make a blizzard in a jar craft. You need a clear plastic or glass jar with a lid, glitter, and foam balls. Construct a snowman out of foam balls, add a fabric scarf, toothpick arms, and draw a face on with a permanent marker. Glue it all together with hot glue. Secure it to the inside of your jar lid with hot glue. Add in glitter to cover the bottom of the jar. Glue on the lid. Just shake it to create a blizzard.

Additional Layer

Wind chill is the perceived temperature on the skin when the effect of the wind is taken into account.

Wind carries heat away from the body more rapidly than it would otherwise be lost.

Learn more about how wind chill is calculated.

Additional Layer

Monsoons are a particularly wet, rainy season in certain tropical parts of the world, especially India, Pakistan, Bangladesh, and West Africa.

Photo by Harsh Mangal, CC license.

The rain is much needed and generally celebrated in these places, but can also cause catastrophic flooding and destruction of life and property.

Monsoons occur when the land temperature is especially high; this means lots of heated air will rise and cooler ocean air will rush into the void, making wind and bringing moisture from the ocean.

ARTS: KING ARTHUR TALES

It's quite possible that more stories have been written about King Arthur and his knights than about any other single subject. Some people think Arthur was an actual historical king and others think he was purely fiction. I'm afraid we can't tell you for sure one way or the other. But if Arthur were real he would have lived just before the time when the Celtic-Romano people were defending themselves and Britain and Christianity from the heathen Barbarian tribes who were in danger of overrunning them. If the tales are true, then Arthur was successful in welding together his countrymen and holding off the invaders during his lifetime, though the British were eventually overrun and pushed into the extreme western part of the British Island, in the area we now call Wales.

The Death of King Arthur by John Garrick, 1862

Britain had been converted to Christianity during the time of the Romans and we know they held on to their faith after the Romans left, but it is interesting that the Arthur stories, while full of Christian faith and symbols, are also full of old pagan magic, sprites, fairies, and wizards. Many of the peoples surrounding them, including the Vikings and their own Celtic ancestors, believed in magic and mystical creatures, so it's not surprising that some of this made its way into their stories.

The Arthur legends were told by word of mouth for almost a thousand years until Sir Thomas Malory, a knight who was being held prisoner, wrote down the tales in the 1470's (or thereabouts). Modern tales of Arthur are based more or less on Malory's writings.

This unit requires reading at least some of the legends. There are many versions encompassing all reading levels from read-aloud picture books to adult versions. See the library list at the beginning of this unit for suggestions. Choose an appropriate one and once you've read the famous legends, choose from the following activities:

Merlin taking away the baby Arthur to hide from his enemies, from "The Boys King Arthur" by N.C. Wyeth.

😊 😊 EXPLORATION: Discussion

Read *The Story of King Arthur and His Knights* by Howard Pyle, *Part One: The Winning of Kinghood* and then discuss the book using the questions below as a guide.

1. What is the setting of the story? Where and when does it take place?
2. Who was your favorite character and why?
3. Howard Pyle, an American, wrote this story in 1902, but he used an archaic form of English more similar to Malory's time than his own. Why do you think he did that?
4. Why did Arthur have to prove himself by pulling the sword from the stone over and over? Did the other kings want a high king?
5. What was Merlin's role? How did he serve Britain?
6. Merlin uses magic to help him in aiding Britain, but the people of the day were Christian, a religion that does not believe in magic. How is this reconciled? Does it seem out of place in the book?
7. How did Arthur treat his older brother, Sir Kay, when it was discovered who Arthur really was? How did Kay respond?
8. How does Arthur show his greatness of character even as a young man?

Famous Folks

The Lady of Shalott, also known as Elaine, was tragically in love with Lancelot. She dies while floating down the river toward Camelot, lying down in an open boat.

Read more about her in Tennyson's *Idylls of the King* and *Lady of Shalott*.

Lady of Shalott by John Grimshaw.

The Lady of Shalott by JW Waterhouse, 1888.

Writer's Workshop

Write about chivalry:

What were the fundamentals of chivalry in the Arthur legends?

What are the advantages and disadvantages of a society that is built on loyalty, honor, and trust?

Is chivalry alive today?

Chivalry wasn't just about a moral code . . . keep reading further.

Writer's Workshop

Pretend you are one of the knights of the round table. Create a professional resume detailing your background, skills, and feats.

Memorization Station

Read *The Lady of Shalott* by Alfred Lord Tennyson and memorize a few of your favorite stanzas.

> *There she weaves by*
> *night and day*
> *A magic web with*
> *colours gay.*
> *She has heard a whisper*
> *say,*
> *A curse is on her if she*
> *stay*
> *To look down to*
> *Camelot.*
> *She knows not what the*
> *curse may be,*
> *And so she weaveth*
> *steadily,*
> *And little other care*
> *hath she,*
> *The Lady of Shalott.*

Additional Layer

After John F. Kennedy died in 1963 people referred to his time in the White House as "Camelot." Why would people have given the Kennedy era that name?

9. This story uses the idea that people born to high office have greater virtue than the average person, but also greater potential for evil. What do you think of this idea?
10. Why were a few of the kings so angry that Arthur won the high kingship? How did Arthur respond to them?
11. Which virtues in the legends are most highly respected? Are they the same virtues we value most today?

☺ ☻ EXPLORATION: The Sword in the Stone

One of the most famous tales of King Arthur is the one where as a child he pulled a sword from a stone.

In some tales the sword was set there by Merlin who knew very well which boy was the true heir to the throne, but in other tales the sword is set into the stone by a mystical invisible hand and can be pulled out only by one who is both the true heir and who is moral and honorable.

The story is that as a baby Arthur had enemies who wanted to kill him. He was hidden by Merlin, the wise sorcerer, until such time as he was old enough to take the throne. While still a teenager, Arthur went to Londonium with his older "brother," Kay, to act as his squire. But Kay misplaced his sword and Arthur, not knowing what to do, saw a sword sticking out of an anvil and stone in the courtyard of a church. He hurried and drew the sword so that Kay would have a weapon for the contest. But when Arthur appeared with the sword Kay immediately knew which sword it was. A great crowd gathered back at the stone and anvil, the sword was replaced and many strong men tried to draw it, but again none could draw it but Arthur. So by this means everyone knew Arthur was the rightful king of England.

What qualities do you think a truly great king should have?

Get a piece of craft foam, florist foam, cut off the corners to make an irregular shape and paint it gray or brown to look like a rock.

Purchase little sword shaped toothpicks from the party store, write a different quality on each and stick it into the "stone."

☺ ☻ ☻ EXPLORATION: Guinevere

The character of Guinevere in the legends depends on the author, but in general, though she is lovely, she is not wholesome. Merlin warns Arthur against marrying her, but Arthur, smitten with her beauty, doesn't listen. Though wed to Arthur, she loves Lancelot and is unfaithful to her husband. In the end her lack of chastity destroys herself, Lancelot, Arthur, and the kingdom.

Lancelot and Guinevere by Herbert James Draper

How does personal virtue affect our happiness and our success? What is your moral code and why? How important is it to associate with people who have good morals?

Make a cone shaped princess hat with streamers coming down from the point. On each streamer write down one quality of a truly great queen, the queen Guinevere should have been.

We used 12" x 12" decorative scrapbook paper, then rolled it into a cone that we sized to fit my daughter's head. Once taped, we just trimmed the uneven bottom to finish the round. We pulled streamers through a small circle at the top and taped them inside the cone.

☺ ☻ EXPLORATION: The Knights of the Round Table
As a wedding gift from his father-in-law, Arthur was given a large round table, so big it could seat up to 150 knights! Each time a new knight joined Arthur's ranks his name magically appeared on the back of his chair at the round table.

Additional Layer
Camelot is King Arthur's castle and the center of his court and knights. It is very unlikely that it was ever a real place, having been invented by 12th century writers. More importantly the castle represents a golden age of peace and prosperity with a little magic thrown in.

Additional Layer
Guinevere was Welsh and Arthur would have been a Celt. Celtic kings and queens ruled together as equals. Guinevere would have had all the same powers as Arthur.

Later medieval writers, influenced by Catholic ideas of a woman's role, would have seen any woman as empowered and involved in the public sphere as an immoral woman.

The tales of Guinevere's infidelity do not appear until relatively later in the story's history. It is possible therefore that the real Guinevere, if there was one, was not unfaithful at all, but only powerful and prominent.

But that's all speculation.

Explanation

When you become your own teacher, when you choose your own books and plan your own projects, learning itself is a creative act.

Creativity is taking the magical bits of the wonders of the world and making them into something that is uniquely us. We don't start with a blank slate. We start with the whole world at our fingertips and realize we have a part to play in that wonder. Creativity is taking what the world has given us and giving a bit back.

At the end of the day, my creativity is there to bring me satisfaction in my work and blessings to the lives of others. I hope that is what I do and I hope that is what I teach my kids; not to get good grades so they can go to a good college so they can get a good job and make good money, but to learn for the adventure of it, to produce for the joy of it, and to help others because we're human and it's what we do.

Michelle

What is the advantage of meeting at a round table rather than a square one? Celtic warriors often met in circles so no one could be at the head, and therefore, superior. Most organizations today, including churches, businesses, and government are based on a hierarchical structure, with a clear line of authority from the top down. Are there other options?

Make a round table craft from a piece of cardboard cut into a round and a square base made from a milk carton or similar packaging. Paint it all out in brown. Write the names of some of Arthur's knights on their places at the table.

☺ ☺ ☺ EXPLORATION: Heroes
Make a presentation about someone who is your hero. You could make a story, write a paper, create a video, make a slide show, or give a speech. Discuss their qualities and what makes them a hero to you. Are any of those qualities the same ones that heroes during the Middle Ages possessed?

☺ ☺ EXPLORATION: Excalibur
Excalibur was the sword of King Arthur. It was thought to be a magical sword and would only work for the rightful king. Its blade was engraved with words. In Tennyson's version one side of the sword said "Take me" and the other side said "Throw me away."

Make a cardboard sword by cutting 2 identical swords out of a large piece of cardboard. Swords were many different shapes, so choose one that suits you. Use tape to secure a long dowel between the two swords for strength, making sure the dowel is long enough to run all the way from the handle down the sword.

Then wrap the two blades together with masking tape all the way around every inch of the sword.

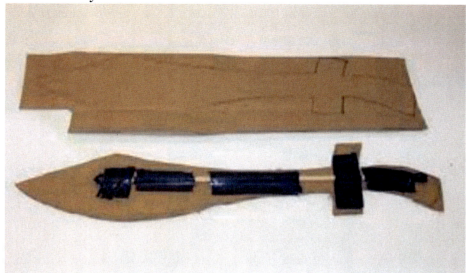

You can either paint your sword, or you can just paint the handle and wrap the blade in aluminum foil and then packaging tape.

If you'd like to, you can use a permanent marker to write your own message on your sword.

☺ ☺ ☺ EXPLORATION: The Holy Grail

Read the preamble to the story of the Legend of the Holy Grail from the end of this unit. Then have the kids each write an adventure that one or several of the knights have during their quest for the Holy Grail. It can be as short as a caption of a picture for the youngest kids or as long as several pages for older kids. Before they write, talk about plot.

Plot is the design of your story, it is the main course of action that a character goes through. It can be actions that a character does or it can be things that happen to the character. There should be one central key event that happens to your character and then supporting events that lead to or from that central event. So if we were to write an adventure for Galahad, we might decide he has a clue toward the grail from an old hermit that tells him he must reach an island in the center of a lake. Galahad making it to the island is the central event, but along the way he might have to find the lake by wandering around or by asking questions of local peasants. A fairy might trick him and try to lead him astray. He might have to fight a wicked knight who is trying to carry off a lady against her will. He might find an enchanted boat at the edge of the lake and decide whether or not to climb into it. Finally, we need to decide what happens when he reaches the

On the Web

Learn more about the world of King Arthur lore at: http://www.kingarthursknights.com/

Fabulous Fact
Indiana Jones and the Last Crusade is a "Holy Grail" story. You can set your story about the Holy Grail anywhere, not just medieval Britain.

Fabulous Fact
The Holy Grail didn't enter into the Arthur stories until several centuries after they began to be written down. At first mention the grail was a dish, and not considered holy. Later it took on mystical qualities and came to be known as a cup, the cup used for the sacrament at Christ's Last Supper.

The Holy Grail appears in the center of the Knights at the Round Table.

Additional Layer

The King Arthur legends are definitely Christian, but they are also Celtic. There are mystical stones, and fairies, and sorceresses, and magic swords, and sacred groves. Why do you think the stories include both Christian and Celtic pagan elements? Do they work together in the stories or does it feel awkward?

Memorization Station

Idylls of the King by Tennyson is a very long poem, expanding on the Arthurian legends. Memorize a few of your favorite stanzas of this beautiful language.

*'Sir Lancelot, as became
a noble knight,
Was gracious to all
ladies, and the same
In open battle or the
tilting-field
Forbore his own
advantage, and the King
In open battle or the
tilting-field
Forbore his own
advantage, and these
two
Were the most nobly-
mannered men of all;
For manners are not
idle, but the fruit
Of loyal nature, and of
noble mind.'*

island (if he does). Is the grail there? Is another clue there? Did the hermit lead him astray? Does he have to fight an ogre? Does he find some of his friends there in an enchanted sleep, but not the grail?

Once you've brainstormed some ideas together, then have each kid write down the elements of plot they want to use on index cards. On the backside of each card, write what happens as a result of that event. The kids can rearrange the cards in any order they like, then write their story.

The choices your character makes should lead to events. Good choices should lead to the correct outcomes and poor choices should lead to incorrect outcomes. But good choices don't necessarily lead to success. For example, Galahad may choose to do the right thing and save the maiden only to find that because he "wasted" time he misses the enchanted boat and must wander for several more years in his quest. On the other hand, he could be made to understand, maybe in a vision, that if he had chosen to leave the maiden to her fate, he would never have found the grail. Remember what Merlin said in the beginning of the story – it is the quest and not the grail itself that is the object. As you give your character hard choices to make, you reveal who he really is at the core.

☺ ☺ ☺ EXPLORATION: WANTED!

Choose one of these characters to create a wanted poster for: Mordred, Lancelot, or Morgan LeFay.

Include this information on your poster:

Who
Wanted for
Reward
Physical Description
Aliases
Known cohorts

This activity helps kids to understand characters in a story. Encourage them to be as thorough as possible. Point out the difference between flat characters and rounded characters. A flat character is all good or all bad, usually with one strong personality trait. A rounded character is mostly good or bad, but with one fatal flaw. A mostly good character may be covetous, tell lies, or be selfish. In a mostly bad character it might be opposite. They 're wicked, but they also save someone from dying, or they always tell the truth, or they keep their promises.

😊 EXPLORATION: Be a King or Queen

Make a king's or queen's crown to wear using colored poster board, markers or paints, and fake jewels or sequins that are glued on. Begin by tracing a repeating design to form the top border of your crown. Hold it up to your head to determine the size and secure with staples. Decorate it any way you'd like!

😊 😊 😊 EXPLORATION: A Knight's Coat of Arms

Arthur's Knights were brave, valiant men. Create a coat of arms that represents you, as one of his knights. The coat of arms would've adorned his banner and his shield.

Use the coat of arms template at the end of this unit. Fill in each section completely, leaving no white space.

In section 1: Draw an animal that represents you. Think about the animal's characteristics and how you have those same qualities.

In section 2: Draw your greatest accomplishment in life.

In section 3: Draw a picture of yourself accomplishing an important goal.

In section 4: Draw your most-prized, favorite possession.

In section 5: Draw a picture of the people you love most in the world.

Famous Folks

In most King Arthur stories Morgan le Fay is Arthur's arch enemy. She is a sorceress and Arthur's half-sister. But in other stories she is a healer and saves Arthur by taking him to the island of Avalon to be healed after he is wounded in battle.

Famous Folks

The Green Knight was enchanted by Morgan le Fay and is sent as a test and a trap for Arthur's knights. He is called the Green Knight because his skin is really green, though this fact is never explained properly.

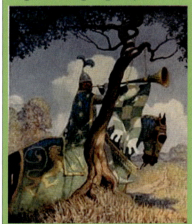

The Green Knight from *The Boys' King Arthur* by N.C. Wythe.

In section 6: Draw a picture of the place you live.

😊 😊 😊 EXPLORATION: Character Sketch

Choose one of the characters you've met in the Arthur tales and create a character sketch. Start by drawing a picture of the person. All around the picture write as much description as you can from what you know. Include both personality, likes and dislikes, and appearance. Remember to include their good qualities as well as their bad. This is what makes a rounded character. Unlike characters in fairy tales, the characters of King Arthur have many facets of their personalities.

An oil painting of Guinivere, by John Collier

😊 😊 EXPLORATION: History or Fantasy? You Decide

Divide a sheet of paper into two columns. At the top of one column, write "History" and at the top of the other "Fantasy." In the first column, write down at least 5 realistic aspects of a King Arthur story you read. In the second column, write down some of the mythical or magical aspects.

After reading the tales and learning about this time period so far, what do you believe? Was Arthur real?

Coming up next . . .

Unit 2-6

Charlemagne - France
Cells & DNA
Carolingian Art

My Ideas For This Unit:

Title: _____   Topic: _____

_____

_____

_____

_____

_____

_____

_____

_____

Title: _____   Topic: _____

_____

_____

_____

_____

_____

_____

_____

_____

Title: _____   Topic: _____

_____

_____

_____

_____

_____

_____

_____

_____

My Ideas For This Unit:

Title: _____   Topic: _____

_____

_____

_____

_____

_____

_____

_____

_____

_____

Title: _____   Topic: _____

_____

_____

_____

_____

_____

_____

_____

_____

_____

_____

Title: _____   Topic: _____

_____

_____

_____

_____

_____

_____

_____

_____

Anglo-Saxons

This is an Anglo-Saxon sword and shield with a dragon on it. The Anglo-Saxons were Danish and Germanic people who invaded England in the unrest after the Romans pulled out of Britain. They were eventually overrun by Viking people, but their descendants still live in England today.

400 AD 2-5

Vortigern of Britain asked for Saxon help in conquering the Picts; they revolt and take his kingdom

410-520 AD 2-5

Angles, Saxons, and Jutes invaded and settled Britain, destroying the Christian religion wherever they settled

Early 500's 2-5

King Arthur united his people in defense of their lands from the invaders. He was successful for a time

597 AD 2-5

Roman Christianity re-introduced by St. Augustine

600 AD 2-5

Britain divided into seven kingdoms

663 AD 2-5

Synod of Whitby decided to accept Roman Christianity over Celtic

716 AD 2-5

Mercian Kingdom dominated the rest of the Saxon kingdoms

757 AD 2-5

Offa, powerful Mercian King ruled

867-874 AD 2-5

The first Danish Viking invasion

871-899 AD 2-5

Alfred was elected King of Wessex, he and his daughter hold back the Vikings

924-939 AD 2-5

Athelstan was King of England

1013-1042 AD 2-5

Danes ruled England

1024-1066 2-5

Edward the Confessor was elected King of England

1066 AD 2-5

William of Normandy conquered England

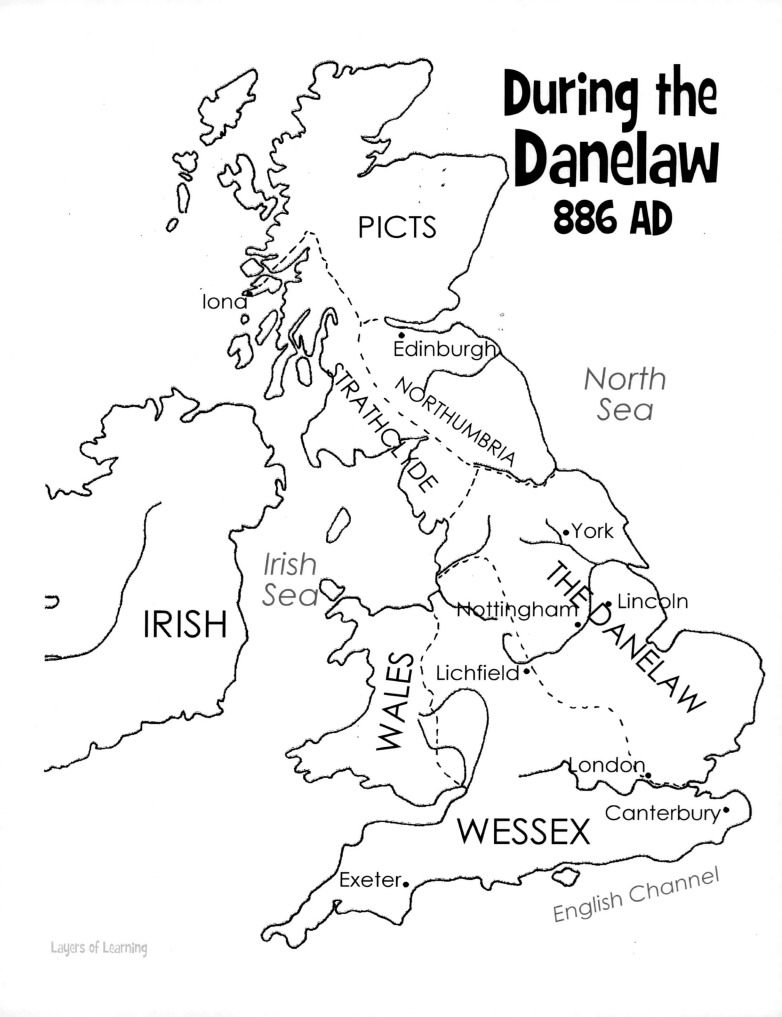

crown

head
covering

cloak

tunic

overdress

seax knife
shows they
are freemen

long underdress

Royalty

Noble

simple tunic

long dress

woolen cloth
wrapped
around legs

bare legs
and feet

Churl

Slave

helmet

chainmail hood

cloak, fastened with a brooch

battle axe

plain tunic

Thane

Monk

Great Britain

Big Ben, The Great Clock, and The Elizabeth Tower

A lot of people think this tower in London is called Big Ben, but that's actually the name of the bells inside the tower that ring. The tower is called the Elizabeth Tower. The clock inside is called the Great Clock.

The Legend of the Holy Grail

The vision faded as quickly as it had appeared, but all the mighty knights seated around the Round Table of Arthur had seen it. For nearly a full minute a cup, wooden and plain, but glowing with a brilliant holy light had floated about four feet off the floor in the center of their circle.

"What does this mean? Merlin?" asked Arthur.

Merlin paused, then slowly got to his feet. Merlin was wise, learned, and close to things spiritual and magical, though Merlin himself never spoke of any of it as magic. For "magic" is the word men use when they do not understand the source.

Merlin began to speak, slow and measured he told this tale, "Legends say that Joseph of Arimathea, the great uncle of the Christ, who gave up his tomb to lay the body of the Son of God, was given a wooden cup used by Jesus at the Last Supper with his apostles. Into the wooden cup had been collected the blood and sweat of Christ, which represents the Love of God and his atonement, as he died upon the cross. Joseph was soon after sealed alive into another tomb of rock, but he kept the cup with him. The cup it turned out was magical; it produced food and drink that kept Joseph alive for several years before his friends could free him. After he was freed, Joseph fled to the British Isles, far from his enemies. As he lay dying he charged that the descendants of his daughter, Anna, brave knights all, should guard and keep the cup secret and safe. But he promised that though the cup would be lost to history, it would one day be found by one of his descendants, the bravest and most virtuous knight in the land. So the knights of St. Joseph have kept the cup, known as the Holy Grail, safe in the Castle of Corbenic until this day. But no man knows where that castle is now. Today we have been given a sign that now is the time to seek after the Grail and we know that he who should take on this quest is seated among us."

All eyes turned toward Arthur, but Arthur was slowly shaking his head. He above all others knew he was not this virtuous, unstained knight the legend spoke of.

"No, my friends it is not Arthur's quest," said Merlin, "Arthur's quest was to build Camelot, secure the borders from the barbarians, and bring peace to this land. The Quest for the Holy Grail falls to Galahad, son of Lancelot, and the knight that joined us only a few days before."

Now all eyes looked at Galahad, who stood and firmly said, "I will go. Must I go alone?"

"No," said Merlin, "You may choose companions to aid you in your quest. Bear in mind they must be loyal, brave, and virtuous or you will fail. This quest will consume many years of your life. For it is possible that it is the quest and not the finding of the Grail that is the testimony of our Christ. But the Grail, it is said, will heal the land."

The knights broke into whispers one with another so that there was a murmur and hissing around the table. Heal the land? Everyone knew that Arthur was aging, that his kingdom, won with so much toil and blood, was already unraveling as people began to grow wicked once a gain. There were enemies without seeking to take over and destroy, but it was the enemies within that would make the kingdom weak and vulnerable. More than the strong arms of a few knights, more even than the brilliant leadership of Arthur or the wisdom of Merlin were needed to hold it all together. They needed to be healed by a miracle.

So Galahad left the Round Table and chose three knights to accompany him: Sir Perceval, Sir Bors, and Sir Gwion, who had once been a kitchen boy.

For many years and through many adventures, crossing from one end of Britain to another, the mighty knights, sometimes joined by one or another of their brethren, and sometimes splitting up to go their separate ways, searched after the Holy Grail and these are some of their adventures.

Coat of Arms

ABOUT THE AUTHORS

Karen & Michelle . . .
Mothers, sisters, teachers, women who are passionate
about educating kids.
We are dedicated to lifelong learning.

Karen, a mother of four, who has homeschooled her kids for more than eight years with her husband, Bob, has a bachelor's degree in child development with an emphasis in education. She lives in Utah where she gardens, teaches piano, and plays an excruciating number of board games with her kids. Karen is our resident Arts expert and English guru {most necessary as Michelle regularly and carelessly mangles the English language and occasionally steps over the bounds of polite society}.

Michelle and her husband, Cameron, homeschooling now for over a decade, teach their six boys on their ten acres in beautiful Idaho country. Michelle earned a bachelors in biology, making her the resident Science expert, though she is mocked by her friends for being the *Botanist with the Black Thumb of Death*. She also is the go-to for History and Government. She believes in staying up late, hot chocolate, and a no whining policy. We both pitch in on Geography, in case you were wondering, and are on a continual quest for knowledge.

Visit our constantly updated blog for tons of free ideas,
free printables, and more cool stuff for sale:
www.Layers-of-Learning.com

Made in the USA
Middletown, DE
04 April 2025